INSTANT MATH STORYMATS

With Hands-on Activities
for Building Essential Primary Math Skills

by Mary Beth Spann

SCHOLASTIC
PROFESSIONAL BOOKS

NEW YORK • TORONTO • LONDON • AUCKLAND • SYDNEY

To my family with all my love.
And to teachers everywhere who strive to bring meaningful
math experiences to the children they teach.
—M.B.S.

ACKNOWLEDGMENTS

My endless gratitude to four incredibly intelligent, talented, and insightful friends and colleagues who helped conceive, develop, and shape this book: Marcia Miller, Mathematics Consultant, New York, NY; Terry Cooper, Editor-in-Chief, Scholastic Professional Books; Liza Charlesworth, Executive Editor, Scholastic Professional Books; Valerie Williams, 1st Grade Teacher, Great Neck, NY. Working with each of you is a joy and a privilege. Thanks also to James Hale for contributing his beautiful artwork. And, finally, special hugs to my 6-year-old daughter, Francesca Spann Minucci, who cheerfully helped me test the storymat games and activities in this book to make certain they would be engaging for other kids her age.

Cover design by Vincent Ceci and Jaime Lucero
Interior design by Solutions by Design, Inc.
Interior illustration by James Graham Hale

Book ISBN 0-590-10109-9

CONTENTS

ABOUT MATH STORYMATS

Welcome to the World of Math Storymats!

This book contains 18 reproducible Math Storymats, each one a refreshing addition to your early elementary math program. Each storymat is accompanied by two separate read-aloud story selections for you to present to your students. These stories guide children in using plastic disk-shaped markers to interact with the mats in specific and open-ended ways. Together, the mats and the manipulatives help children explore and practice math skills and concepts. As you observe your children manipulating markers on the mat, you gain insight into their ability to employ math strategies in performing activities or solving problems. Because the mats are versatile enough to use in an individual, small, or large group setting, there are lots of opportunities for you to engage in "math talk" with your students.

Fitting Math Storymats into the Curriculum

No matter what math materials and manipulatives you rely on now, there's room in your day for math storymats. They're easy to use, require almost no preparation, and provide a period of math fun for children.

You can schedule a math storymat activity whenever you like and keep an activity going for as much or as little time as you need. You can extend and deepen any math storymat activity by posing open-ended questions (or by encouraging students to do the same). Each read-aloud story is accompanied by Math Talk Tips designed to foster further math discussions and explorations. You also might try asking:

- ☼ What if . . . ?
- ☼ I wonder what would happen if we . . . ?
- ☼ Can you think of another way to show . . . ?
- ☼ I see you have arrived at two different ways to do this problem. Does anyone have another way?
- ☼ Can you help us understand how you . . . ?

Grouping Students for Storymats

Math Storymats are designed to be used with any number of students. While we flagged a number of mats that can be presented to a whole class (requiring only the number of markers packaged with this book), all 18 mats are appropriate for use with small groups of children or with individual students. Additional markers can be ordered from Learning Resources by calling 1-800-222-3909.

What are the benefits of each grouping arrangement? A whole group activity is the most convenient approach—it allows you to pack a lot of math into a short time span for the maximum number of students. Small groupings let you glean-at-a-glance the math skills and strategies your children employ, while also encouraging intimate math conversations. And finally, individualized math sessions (with one child at a time) can give you an up-close peek into each child's growing math abilities, plus the chance to dialogue and assess how that child thinks mathematically. We suggest you try experimenting with different grouping arrangements to discover how these storymats can work best for you and your students.

No One Right Way

Children of all ability levels love using math storymats because there is no one right way to get any one answer. Children in the same group or class may discover many new and different ways to understand or express the same concept. Math storymats' emphasis is on exploring math and respecting process—not on mastery or correctness. With this attitude inherent in the materials themselves, it's easy to respect each child as a learner and each answer as the learner's attempt to discover a truth. Keep in mind, children who are encouraged to guess, wonder, and experiment in math are not afraid to learn because they know they cannot fail.

HOW TO USE THIS BOOK

Everything in math storymats has been organized for you. Each reproducible storymat is accompanied by guides to two different activities. Each guide comprises:

- *Target Skills* children will be addressing when working out the activity, game, or problem on the mat. (In addition to the skills listed, all of the activities involve listening and following directions, and many also involve color recognition.)

- *Materials List.* For nearly all the sessions, children need only the storymat, the specified or suggested number of markers, and containers. (Small margarine tubs or cups work well.) The number of markers given is "per child," but for some activities you may find it more desirable or practical to have groups of children working together as a unit with the given number of markers. Usually, though, you will find it helpful to place each child's markers into an individual cup before beginning an activity.

- *Steps* to get you started using the activity.

- *Read-Aloud Story* consisting of a brief text to be read to the children. This presents the activity, game, or problem and tells the children how to approach it. Since the information here is crucial to the storymat, you will want to read it slowly, emphasizing the key points, and in some cases perhaps repeat it more than the suggested two times.

- *Math Talk Tips* to help you recognize and make the most of math conversation opportunities.

- *Journal Extensions* featuring suggestions for helping children reflect on what they've learned and respond to it in writing and/or with illustrations. Journal responses are open-ended: each one will reflect the developmental levels (both in areas of writing skills and math conceptualization) of the individual child.

You are encouraged to read through the pages accompanying each mat before presenting the mat and corresponding activities to your students. Because most of the read-aloud stories have an open-ended quality to them (that is, they pose invitations for children to use the mats and markers in different ways to solve problems, demonstrate concepts, or just add their own special touch to a mat), you can try almost any mat at almost any time. Other times, you may want to select mats that most closely link up with themes, concepts, or skills your students are exploring elsewhere in your curriculum. For example, if you are exploring money concepts, students may especially relish tackling a mat that asks them to manipulate monetary amounts. Also, keep in mind that each math mat can be used in a variety of ways. For example, with a bit of experimentation, you can easily vary the number or colors of markers used with each activity from those originally suggested.

Preparing Math Storymats for Use

To make mat copies more attractive and durable, you may want to color, mount, and laminate them before use, but this is optional. If you wish, students may color in the mats before laminating, or you may copy each mat directly onto heavyweight plain or colored paper. In addition, the back of each math storymat may double as the journal page, pairing a visual reminder of the original mat activity (i.e. the mat itself) with a related journal entry.

Encouraging Student Ideas

The interactive feature of teacher-directed math storymat activities guarantees student participation and input. But be aware that students can also step outside this lesson structure to work out their own story and game scenarios. Encouraging such student's involvement is best done immediately after a teacher-directed math storymat session. This is when children are most familiar with the mat's possibilities, are in a math mindset, and are most ready to play with their own ideas.

One Last Word

Have fun with your math storymats and markers. We know they will become an indispensable math resource you and your students will enjoy using again and again.

	Position	Order	Sorting	Size	Counting	Skip Counting	Addition	Subtraction	Multiplication	Division	Matching	Shapes/Geometry	Comparing Numbers	Patterning	Measurement	Estimation	Fractions	Money	Probability	Graphing	Reasoning
STORY MAT 1	✓	✓					✓				✓	✓									
STORY MAT 2	✓		✓		✓					✓	✓										
STORY MAT 3	✓	✓		✓	✓		✓	✓					✓								
STORY MAT 4	✓	✓			✓		✓	✓			✓		✓	✓	✓						
STORY MAT 5		✓		✓	✓		✓	✓					✓	✓	✓	✓	✓				
STORY MAT 6	✓	✓		✓	✓		✓	✓					✓	✓	✓	✓					
STORY MAT 7			✓		✓	✓	✓		✓	✓	✓		✓	✓							
STORY MAT 8	✓	✓		✓	✓								✓	✓		✓	✓				
STORY MAT 9		✓		✓	✓	✓	✓	✓		✓	✓		✓	✓							
STORY MAT 10	✓	✓		✓	✓		✓	✓					✓								
STORY MAT 11	✓	✓	✓		✓								✓								✓
STORY MAT 12	✓				✓	✓	✓	✓	✓				✓								✓
STORY MAT 13		✓			✓	✓	✓	✓					✓		✓		✓				✓
STORY MAT 14			✓		✓		✓	✓					✓					✓			✓
STORY MAT 15	✓	✓		✓	✓		✓	✓					✓	✓					✓		✓
STORY MAT 16	✓				✓	✓	✓		✓	✓			✓			✓					
STORY MAT 17	✓				✓	✓	✓	✓		✓			✓								
STORY MAT 18	✓				✓	✓					✓	✓								✓	✓

On the Playground

ACTIVITY A: ORDER, GEOMETRY

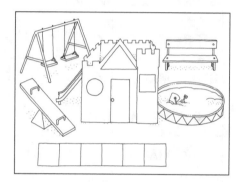

Target Skills

- ◎ position
- ◎ order
- ◎ geometry

Materials

- ◎ copies of Math Storymat 1
- ◎ 6 markers (one of each color) per child

Steps

1 Distribute mats and markers.

2 Have the children just listen as you read the story through once.

3 Read the story through a second time; have children use the markers to "act out" the story as it unfolds.

4 Read the story through a third time; have each child use markers to show new and different hiding spots from the ones originally chosen.

Read-Aloud Story

One fine day, Ms. Sunshine led her class in a straight line along the sidewalk until they stopped at the entrance to the playground. First in line was Ms. Sunshine dressed in yellow. Second was a child dressed in orange, followed by a third child dressed in red, a fourth in blue, a fifth in green, and the last in purple. "Let's play 'Hide and Go Seek'," said Ms. Sunshine. "I will close my eyes and count while you find places to hide." Then Ms. Sunshine walked across the playground, sat on the bench, closed her eyes, and began counting as her children entered the playground and went every which way looking for places to hide. The child dressed in orange hid under a big triangle. The child dressed in red hid in a circle. The child dressed in blue hid above a square. The child dressed in green hid next to a rectangle. And the child dressed in purple hid between two different shapes. Can you describe where Ms. Sunshine found each of the children on your playground mat? Use a marker to show where you would hide.

Math Talk Tip

- At the end of the story, ask the children to clear their mats and then return each of their markers to a different hiding place. Then have children describe specifically where each of their colored markers is hiding. Encourage children to use shape and position words as much as possible.

Journal Extension

Have children use shape and position words to describe where they would hide on the playground.

ACTIVITY B: MATCHING, ADDITION

Target Skills

- position
- order
- matching objects
- basic number facts (addition)

Materials

- copies of Math Storymat 1
- at least 16 markers of mixed colors per child

Steps

1 Distribute mats; place markers within easy reach.

2 Have the children just listen as you read the story through once.

3 Read the story through a second time. Have children use the markers to "act out" the story as it unfolds.

Read-Aloud Story

Today the playground is very crowded. Two grown-ups are on the bench. Two children are riding on the seesaw. Three children are playing in the sand box. The swingset is full. But the play castle is the most crowded of all! Pick your favorite colored marker and put yourself somewhere on the playground.

Math Talk Tips

- It's likely children will each use a different number of markers to interpret "The swingset is full." After working out the story, talk about the different interpretations that emerged. Did the word "full" mean the same thing to each child? This may also be a good time to bring up playground safety issues (e.g., is it a good idea to stand on top of a swingset?).

- Talk with children about how they showed that the play castle is "the most crowded of all" spots in the playground. Ask them to tell how they know. Consider listing the different solutions they settled on.

Journal Extension

Challenge children to count and then write a sentence telling how many children are playing in the playground altogether.

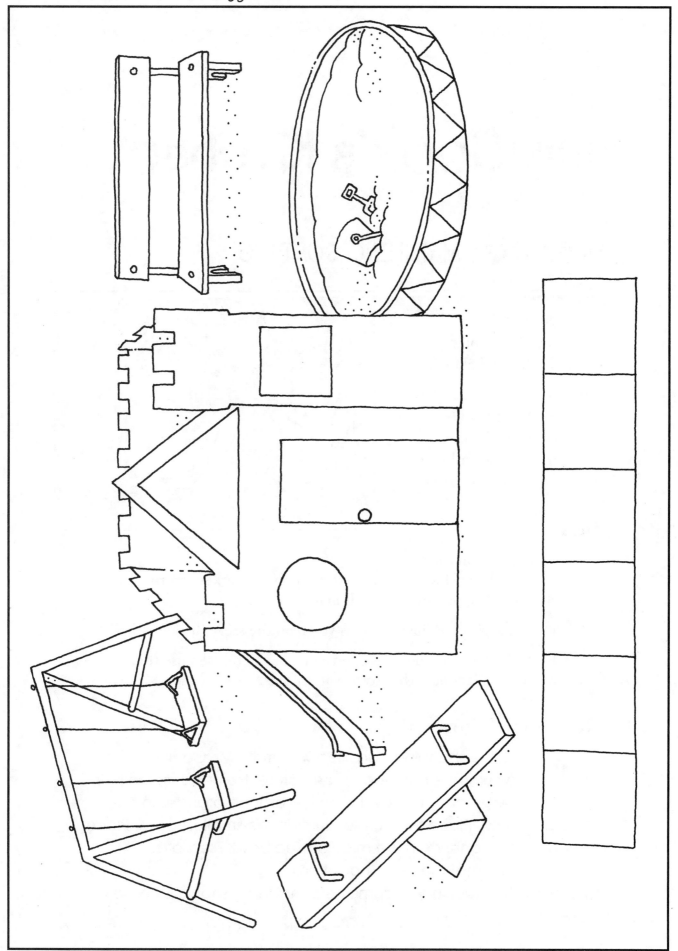

Mr. Cook's Kitchen

ACTIVITY A: MATCHING, SORTING

Target Skills
- ☼ position
- ☼ matching objects
- ☼ sorting and classifying

Materials
- ☼ copies of Math Storymat 2
- ☼ 6 orange, 4 yellow, and 2 purple markers per child

Steps

1 Distribute mats and markers; have children place their supply of markers on the shopping bag pictured on each mat.

2 Have the children just listen as you read the story through once.

3 Read the story through a second time; have children use the markers to "act out" the story as it unfolds.

Read-Aloud Story

☺ See the shopping bag filled with fruit? Mr. Cook has just come home from the grocery store. He needs some help putting his groceries away. Place the orange oranges in the largest bowl. Place the purple plums in the smallest bowl. Place the yellow bananas in the middle-sized bowl. Please don't overlap the mat markers. Thank you.

Now Mr. Cook needs some help making a snack. Choose

<u>some</u> fruits you think he would like to eat and place them on one of Mr. Cook's plates on the table. Count how many fruits are left. Then choose a snack for yourself from the bowls and place it in the shopping bag so you can take it home with you. How many pieces of fruit are left over?

Math Talk Tips + − x ÷ + − x ÷ + − x ÷ + − x ÷ + − x ÷ + − x ÷ + − x ÷ + − x ÷ + −

- ☺ As children work at sorting and placing markers on the mat, ask them to describe how they decided to arrange their markers as they did. (Encourage children to arrange markers so they don't overlap.)

- ☺ Have children count the number of markers representing each piece of food in each category.

- ☺ Ask children to tell about the different kinds and numbers of snacks they chose for Mr. Cook and for themselves. Also, ask them each to tell when they think Mr. Cook will need to shop again.

Journal Extension

Have children each draw a picture and then write a sentence telling one way they might sort the fruits in the story. For example, fruits may be sorted according to color, taste, those you can eat with skin/without skin, and so forth.

ACTIVITY B: COUNTING, DIVISION

Target Skills
- ☺ position
- ☺ matching objects
- ☺ counting
- ☺ basic number facts (division)

Materials
- ☺ copies of Math Storymat 2
- ☺ 6 orange, 4 yellow, and 2 purple markers per child

Steps
1 Distribute mats and markers.

2 Have the children just listen as you read the story through once.

3 Read the story through a second time; have children use the markers to "act out" the story as it unfolds.

Read-Aloud Story

Mr. Cook is having a friend over for dinner. He wants to share <u>all</u> of his fruits so he and his friend *each* have the same amount. He checks the bowls on his counter. He has six orange oranges in the largest bowl. He has two purple plums in the smallest bowl. And he has four yellow bananas in the middle-sized bowl. Can you share each kind of fruit between the two friends? Put their fruits on the two plates on the table. How many of each kind of fruit does each friend have?

Math Talk Tip

⚙ Ask children to describe and/or demonstrate how they were able to divide up the fruits evenly between the two plates. Or, you might do this for them saying, for example, "I noticed you divided your oranges like this. Why did you do it this way? How did you know that would be a good way to divide the six oranges between the two friends?" Use such a discussion to help children see that there may be more than one way to get to the same result.

Journal Extension

Ask children to use the back of the math mat to draw a picture showing how they would divide three apples among two friends. Then have them write a sentence explaining their reasoning.

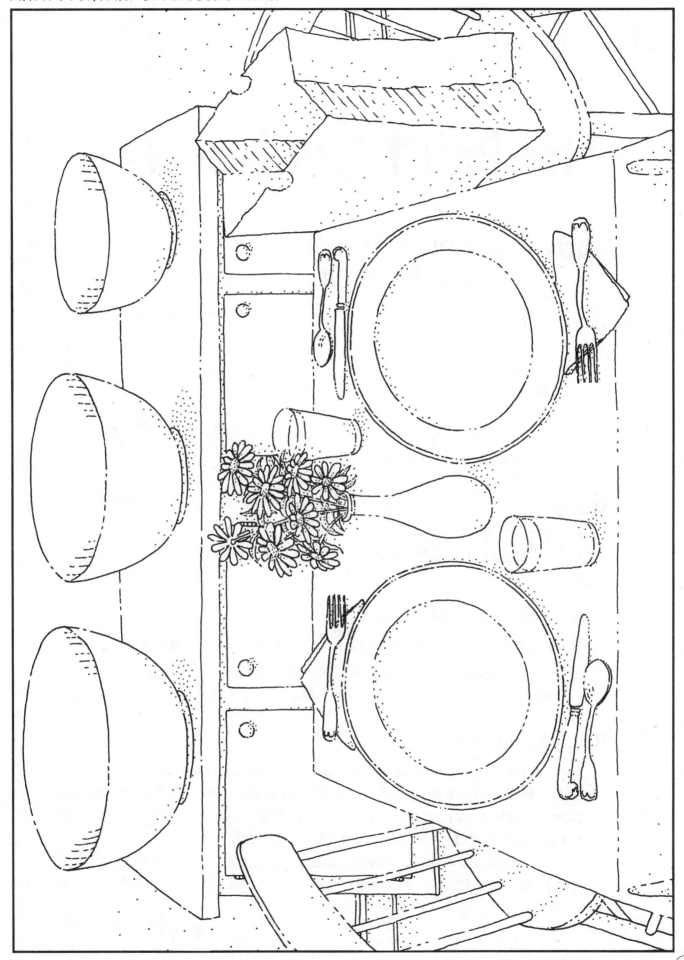

The Fruit Orchard

ACTIVITY A: COUNTING, ADDITION, SUBTRACTION

Target Skills

- ☼ size
- ☼ position
- ☼ order
- ☼ counting
- ☼ comparing numbers
- ☼ basic number facts (addition, subtraction)

Materials

- ☼ copies of Math Storymat 3
- ☼ 7 yellow, 6 red, and 5 orange markers per child

Steps

1 Distribute mats and markers.

2 Have the children just listen as you read the story through once.

3 Read the story through a second time; have children use the markers to "act out" the story as it unfolds.

Read-Aloud Story

☺ Once upon a time there was a young farmer named Matt. One sunny day, he planted three different fruit trees side-by-side in an orchard. Do you see them? Then Matt cared for the trees and he watched and he waited.

Sure enough, it wasn't long before fruit began to appear on the trees. On Monday, Matt noticed three red apples on the

biggest tree, two orange peaches on the middle-sized tree, and
four yellow lemons on the smallest tree. On Tuesday, he noticed
two more apples on the biggest tree, one more peach on the
middle-sized tree, and two more lemons on the smallest tree.
On Wednesday, he noticed there were six apples in all on the
biggest tree, five peaches in all on the middle-sized tree, and
seven lemons in all on the smallest tree. Matt decided to begin
picking the fruit. He wanted some for a snack <u>and</u> he wanted
to leave five pieces of fruit on each tree. How many fruits did
Matt pick altogether? Which fruit was he unable to pick?

Math Talk Tip

- Have children take turns explaining what they needed to do in
  order to leave five fruits on each tree. Encourage children to
  describe what they did using number names and math action words
  like "take away" or "subtract."

Journal Extension

Ask children to tell how they figured out how many fruits the farmer picked
from the trees. Encourage a number of responses representing a number of
different methods (e.g., counting, adding, etc.)

ACTIVITY B: COUNTING, ADDITION, SUBTRACTION

Target Skills

- order
- counting
- comparing numbers
- basic number facts (addition, subtraction)

Materials

- copies of Math Storymat 3
- at least 12 red markers per child
- one number die per child

Steps

1 Distribute mats and markers.

2 Have the children just listen as you read the story through once.

3 Read the story through a second time; have children use the markers and dice to play the game presented.

Read-Aloud Story

One day, a farmer named Liza went to the apple orchard to see if the apples growing there were ready to pick. Sure enough, Liza found three trees brimming with juicy ripe apples. On the first and smallest tree she counted three apples. On the middle-sized tree she counted four apples and on the largest tree she counted five apples. "That looks like a lot of apples altogether. I think I'll make a game out of this apple picking chore," thought Farmer Liza. So she took a die out of her pocket. "Whatever number comes up when I roll this die will tell me how many apples to pick," she said to herself. "I will try and roll the exact numbers I need until I've picked all the apples."

On her first try Liza rolled a two, so she picked two apples. On her second try the number "one" came up, so she picked one apple. "I wonder what number I need to pick all the rest of the apples?" she thought. Help Farmer Liza figure out that number. Now try rolling the dice to get that number so Liza can pick the rest of her fruit. How many tries did you need to take?

Math Talk Tip + − x ÷ + − x ÷ + − x ÷ + − x ÷ + − x ÷ + − x ÷ + − x ÷ + −

❀ At the beginning of the game, ask children to tell the total number of apples on all the trees. Ask them to tell which tree has the most and which has the least number of apples.

Journal Extension

Have children take nine "red apple" markers and divide them evenly among the three trees. Have children use a red crayon to circle each marker before removing it from the mat. Then have them turn the paper over and write a sentence describing how they decided to divide up the apples.

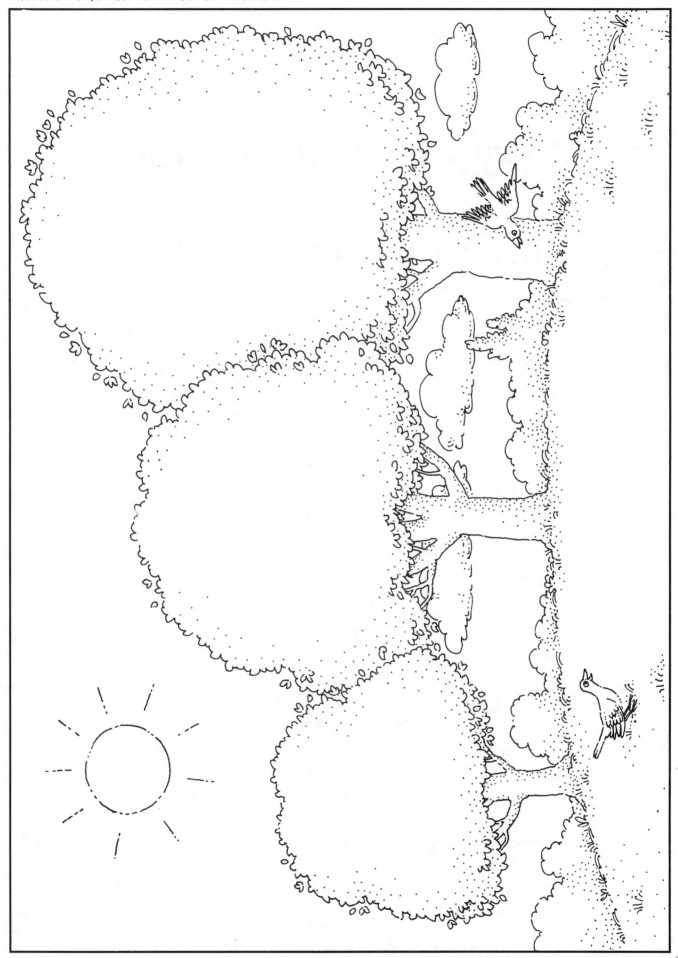

A Walk in The Woods

ACTIVITY A: PATTERNING, COUNTING

Target Skills

- ☀ position
- ☀ order
- ☀ patterns
- ☀ matching
- ☀ counting
- ☀ comparing numbers

Materials

- ☀ copies of Math Storymat 4
- ☀ large supply of markers (at least 10 of each color) per child

Steps

1 Distribute mats and markers.

2 Have the children just listen as you read the story through once.

3 Read the story through a second time; have children use the markers to play the game presented.

Read-Aloud Story

 Little Red Riding Hood is trying to walk through the deep, dark woods to get to Grandma's house. Use your finger to find the stepping-stone path. Reach into the container and pick out two different colored markers. Place the first marker on the first stepping-stone nearest Red's house. Then place the other marker on the stepping-stone next to the first one. This is the beginning of your stepping-stone color pattern.

Now you must continue to pick the same two colors in the

same order to help Red move along. (You must pick without looking.) If you pick a color marker that comes next in your pattern, place it on your mat. If you pick a color that does not come next in your pattern, place it back in the container and try again. Count how many tries it takes you to get Red to Grandma's. Play again to see if you can build the path in a smaller number of tries.

Math Talk Tips

◎ Encourage children to talk about the patterns they are building by wondering aloud with them what color they hope to pick on their next try.

◎ Show children how they may use tally marks to keep track of the number of tries it takes to get to Grandma's.

Journal Extension

Ask children to write sentences describing (or to draw pictures illustrating) the color patterns they built.

ACTIVITY B: MEASUREMENT, COUNTING

Target Skills

◎ position
◎ order
◎ patterns
◎ color matching
◎ counting
◎ comparing numbers
◎ nonstandard measurement

Materials

◎ copies of Math Storymat 4
◎ large supply of markers (12 each of 3 colors) per child

Steps

1 Distribute mats and markers.

2 Have the children just listen as you read the story through once.

3 Read the story through a second time; have children use the markers to play the game presented.

Read-Aloud Story

Red is still trying to get to Grandma's house. This time you will help her by making paths through the woods. Reach into the container and choose three different colored markers. Place one marker on the first stepping-stone in the stone path to Grandma's. Place one marker on the first flower in the flower path. Place one marker on the first leaf in the leaf path. Now, without peeking, take another marker from the container. Place it next to the marker it matches. Keep on taking markers and matching them with your paths, See which color path will stretch from Red's to Grandma's first. Keep playing until all three color paths reach from Red's to Grandma's. Which color path is the longest? Which color path is the shortest?

Math Talk Tip + − x ÷ + − x ÷ + − x ÷ + − x ÷ + − x ÷ + − x ÷ + − x ÷ + − x ÷ + −

◉ As they work, ask children to anticipate which of their paths they believe will reach Grandma's first—and encourage them to explain why they believe as they do. To help them estimate ask, "How many more rocks (or flowers or leaves) do you have to cover?"

Journal Extension

Have children write a sentence using numbers that represent the total number of markers used to mark the three complete paths to Grandma's.

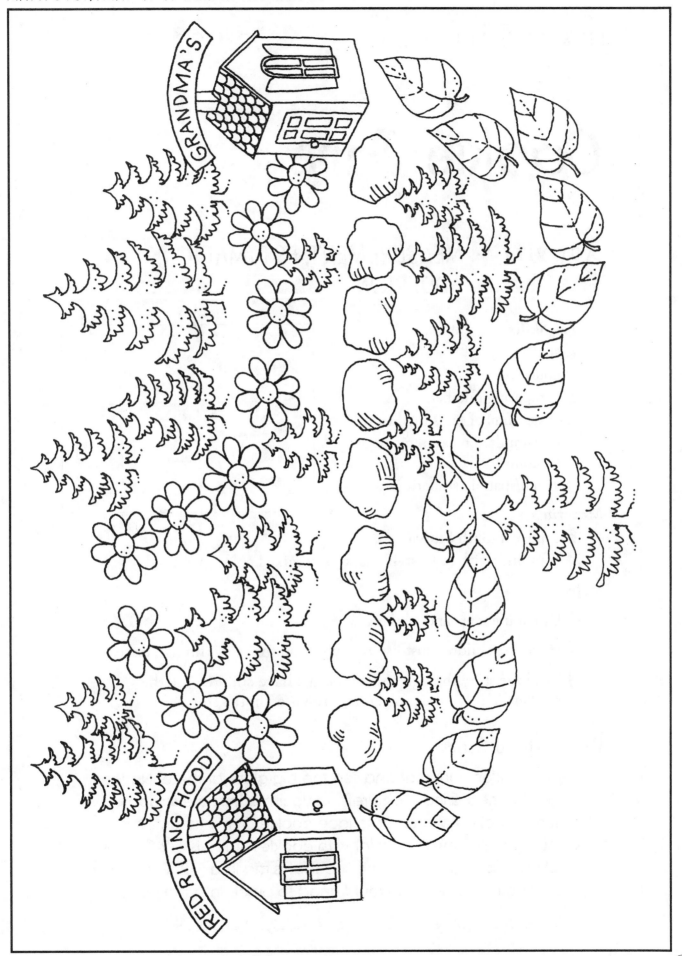

GRANDMA'S

RED RIDING HOOD

Cookie Jars

ACTIVITY A: MEASUREMENT, ESTIMATION, ADDITION

Target Skills

- size
- counting
- comparing numbers
- basic number facts (addition)
- nonstandard measurement (volume)
- visual/spatial estimating

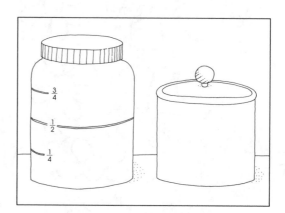

Materials

- copies of Math Storymat 5
- container with at least 40 markers of mixed colors per child

Steps

1 Distribute mats and markers.

2 Have the children just listen as you read the story through once.

3 Read the story through a second time; have children use the markers to solve the problem(s) presented in the story.

Read-Aloud Story

Look on your mat and see the big glass jar there. Notice the measuring lines. Pretend your markers are rainbow-colored cookies. Watch as I place cookies in my jar until it is about 1/2 full. Now fill your jar with cookies until it is 1/2 full. Your cookies must reach up to the line that is marked 1/2. Guess how many more cookies you would need to place into the jar so it is filled to the top. Count out that number of cookies. Then add them to your jar. Did you guess too many cookies, too few cookies, or just the right amount of cookies to fill your jar to the top?

Math Talk Tip $+ - \times \div + - \times \div + - \times \div + - \times \div + - \times \div + - \times \div + - \times \div + - \times \div + -$

- Be aware that because the markers are round, there may be a slight discrepancy among the number of markers in each half jar. Discuss this situation as necessary.

Journal Extension

At the point in the activity when children are asked to estimate how many more markers they will need to fill the jar, stop and ask children to write or draw a journal entry explaining the reasoning behind their guesses.

Have children repeat the math mat activity using the smaller cookie jar. Invite them to use their journals to record the results.

ACTIVITY B: PATTERNING, ESTIMATION, ADDITION, SUBTRACTION

Target Skills

- size
- order
- patterns
- counting
- comparing numbers
- basic number facts (addition, subtraction)
- estimating with fractions

Materials

- copies of Math Storymat 5
- container with at least 16 markers of mixed colors per child

Steps

1 Distribute mats and markers.

2 Have the children just listen as you read the story through once.

3 Read the story through a second time; have children use the markers to "act out" the story as it unfolds.

Read-Aloud Story

Next Friday, James is having a party. All of his friends are coming and James knows just what treats he's going to serve: homemade cookies! When his baking is done, James has enough cookies to fill his small jar. Use your markers to show James's small jar filled with cookies.

A jar full of cookies should be enough for his party. But James's jar doesn't stay full for very long. On Monday he eats four cookies; on Tuesday he eats three cookies; on Wednesday he eats two cookies; on Thursday he eats one cookie. How many cookies does James have left to share with his friends who are visiting on Friday?

Math Talk Tips + – x ÷ + – x ÷ + – x ÷ + – x ÷ + – x ÷ + – x ÷ + – x ÷ + –

- Ask children if they notice a pattern to the number of cookies James eats. Have them describe the pattern and predict what will come next.

- If you have the children repeat the activity using the big jar (as suggested in the Journal Extension below) have them estimate how many mat marker cookies they will need to reach the 1/2 full mark.

Journal Extension

Have children write the subtraction parts of the story as a number sentence (or series of number sentences).

Ask children to use their journals to tell how many cookies James had when his jar was full and how many more he will need to add to his jar so it will be full again.

Have children repeat the math mat activity using the big cookie jar. Invite them to use their journals to record the results.

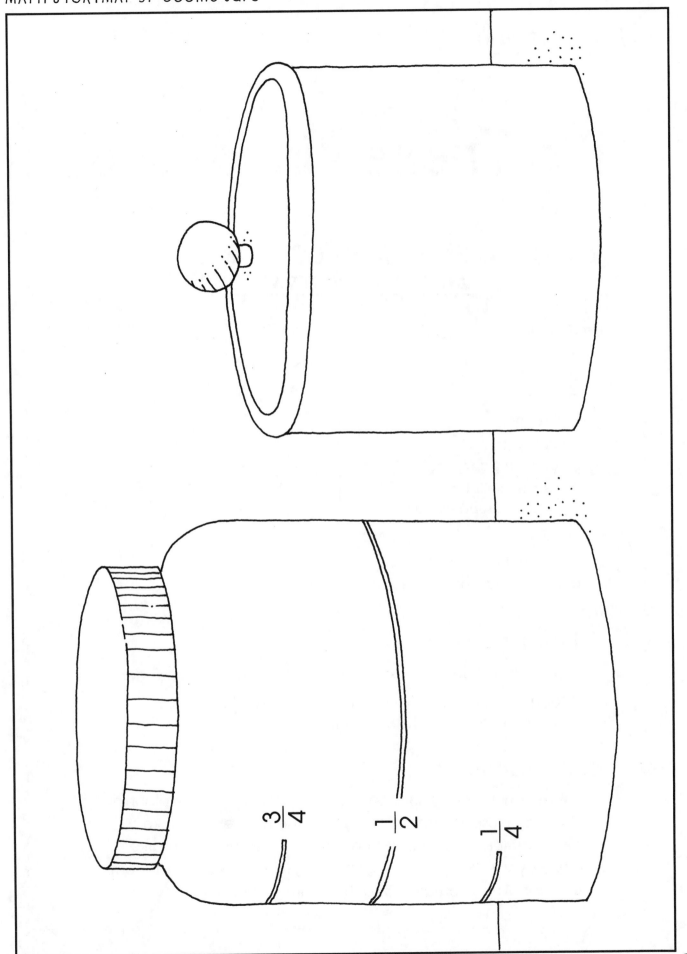

$\frac{3}{4}$

$\frac{1}{2}$

$\frac{1}{4}$

Dig These Dinosaurs!

ACTIVITY A: PATTERNING, COUNTING, ADDITION, SUBTRACTION

Target Skills

Great for the whole class!

- ✷ size
- ✷ position
- ✷ order
- ✷ patterns
- ✷ counting
- ✷ comparing numbers
- ✷ basic number facts (addition, subtraction)

Materials

- ✷ copies of Math Storymat 6
- ✷ at least 15 markers of mixed colors per child

Steps

1 Distribute mats and markers.

2 Have the children just listen as you read the story through once.

3 Read the story through a second time; have children use the markers to "act out" the story as it unfolds.

Read-Aloud Story

☀ Danisha Dinosaur and her little brother Dan are planning a dinosaur birthday party. Use the markers to make a party hat for Danisha and one for Dan. Then use the markers any way you wish to make something fancy for each of them to wear. When you are done, take turns describing how you decorated Danisha and Dan. Be sure to tell how many markers you used.

Math Talk Tip + − x ÷ + − x ÷ + − x ÷ + − x ÷ + − x ÷ + − x ÷ + − x ÷ + −

- ☼ As the children work to dress the dinosaurs, call attention to the various ways the children approached the same task. ("Oh, I see Marcia has used three blue markers to create a necklace for Danisha while Arnold used two different-colored markers to make her necklace!")

Journal Extension

Have children describe the color, number, and arrangement of markers they each used to create a hat for Danisha and a cap for Dan.

ACTIVITY B: ESTIMATION, MEASUREMENT

Target Skills

- ☼ counting
- ☼ estimating
- ☼ comparing numbers
- ☼ basic number facts (addition, subtraction)
- ☼ nonstandard measurement (length, volume)

Great for the whole class!

Materials

- ☼ copies of Math Storymat 6
- ☼ container with at least 12 markers of different colors per child

Steps

1 Distribute mats and markers.

2 Have the children just listen as you read the story through once.

3 Read the story through a second time; have children use the markers to "act out" the story as it unfolds.

Read-Aloud Story

Danisha Dinosaur and her little brother Dan are holding up their feet to try and see who has longer feet. They need your help. You can use the markers to measure. First, watch as I use my mat and markers to show you how to place the markers along the foot Danisha is holding up. Now place your markers along Danisha's foot on your mat. Next, guess how many markers long Dan's foot is. Now measure Dan's foot with the markers and count them to see how well you guessed. Which dinosaur's foot is longer? How do you know? How many more markers did you need to measure the long foot than the short foot?

Math Talk Tip

☸ After you show children how to measure the two dinosaurs' feet, ask them to go through the same process with other body parts: head, arm, whole body, and so forth. Each time, encourage them to share the reasoning behind their estimations.

Journal Extension

Have children write a sentence or draw a picture estimating how many markers would be needed to cover Danisha (or Dan) from head to toe. Have them explain their reasoning.

Dan

Danisha

Let's Picnic!

ACTIVITY A: PATTERNING, SKIP COUNTING

Great for the whole class!

Target Skills
- patterns
- matching objects
- counting
- skip counting
- basic number facts (addition, multiplication)

Materials
- copies of Math Storymat 7
- at least 2 each of orange, green, purple, and yellow markers per child

Steps

1 Distribute mats and markers.

2 Have the children just listen as you read the story through once.

3 Read the story through a second time; have children use the markers to "act out" the story as it unfolds.

Read-Aloud Story

Two friends named Terry and Valerie are planning to share a picnic lunch. They have already passed out the plates, but they still need your help getting ready. The orange markers are cups. Please set out one cup for each friend. The green markers are napkins. Please set out one napkin for each friend. The purple markers are forks. Please set out one fork for each friend. The yellow markers are spoons. Please set out one spoon for each friend. Check to make sure that each place setting on your picnic blanket has an orange cup, a green napkin, a purple fork, and a yellow spoon. How many place settings have you arranged on your blanket? How many markers are in each setting? How many markers are on the whole blanket? Do you notice any color patterns in the arrangement? Now Terry and Valerie are ready to eat!

Math Talk Tips + ÷ x ÷ + ÷ x ÷ + ÷ x ÷ + ÷ x ÷ + ÷ x ÷ + ÷ x ÷ + ÷ x ÷ + ÷ x ÷ + ÷

- ✿ Show children how they may count the total number of markers by skip counting (in groups of two by color or in groups of four by place setting). Also, talk with children about where on the mat they placed their markers. Use position words and phrases such as, next to, above, to the left of, on, etc.

Journal Extension

Have children describe how they arrived at the sum total of markers on the blanket. Then compare answers to see if there is more than one way to total up the markers.

....

ACTIVITY B: PATTERNING, COUNTING, ADDITION

Target Skills
- ✿ matching
- ✿ sorting
- ✿ patterning
- ✿ counting
- ✿ comparing numbers
- ✿ basic number facts (addition)

Materials
- ✿ copies of Math Storymat 7
- ✿ 6 purple, 4 yellow, and 2 orange markers per child

Steps

1 Distribute mats and markers.

2 Have the children mix up the markers and place their markers "in" the picnic basket.

3 Have the children just listen as you read the story through once.

4 Read the story through a second time; have children use the markers to play the game presented.

Read-Aloud Story

Here's a picnic guessing game. For this game, pretend that the markers are really pieces of picnic foods that have become mixed up in your basket. Take the markers out of your picnic basket and spread them out on your picnic blanket. There are four bananas. What color are the bananas? Find the bananas. There are six plums. What color are the plums? Find the plums. There are two cookies. Without moving the markers, find the cookies. What color are the cookies? Can you arrange your markers so that you can easily count how many of each type of food you have on your picnic blanket? Now can you place the food on the plates so the two friends each have the same number of bananas, plums, and cookies?

Math Talk Tip + - x ÷ + - x ÷ + - x ÷ + - x ÷ + - x ÷ + - x ÷ + - x ÷ + -

❂ As children work, ask them to tell which color marker represents which food type. Also, at the story's conclusion, ask them to decide how many pieces of food they have altogether (on each blanket).

Journal Extension

Have children draw a picture showing how they arranged the markers so that they were easy to count.

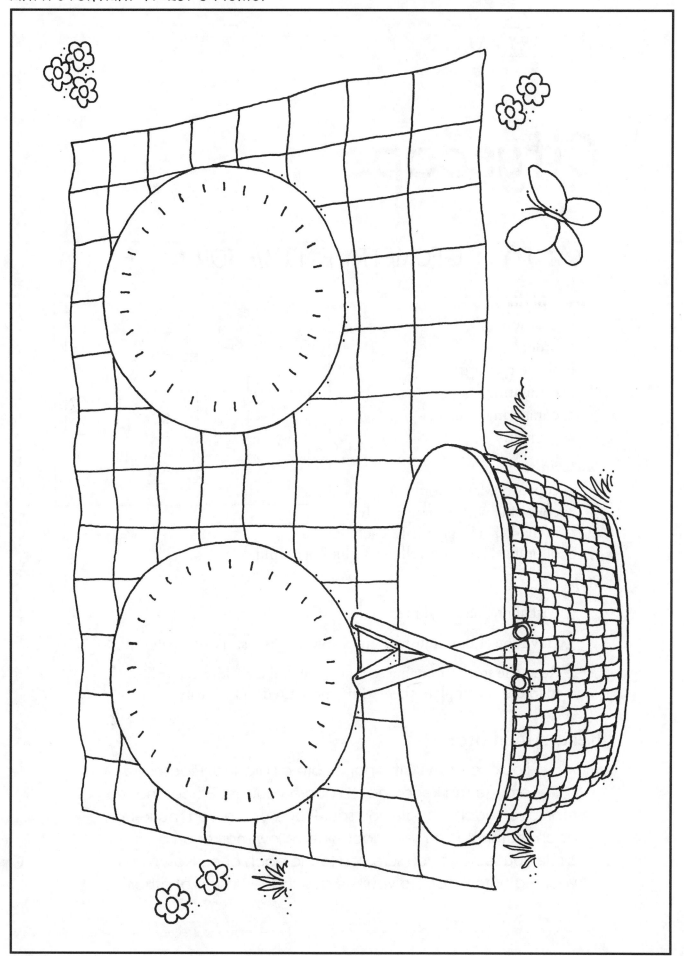

Cityscape

ACTIVITY A: GEOMETRY, ESTIMATION

Target Skills

- position
- order
- shape recognition
- estimating
- comparing numbers
- geometry

Materials

- copies of Math Storymat 8
- container with a large supply of markers (18 green; 12 each of orange, red, and yellow; 3 blue) per child

Steps

1 Distribute mats and markers.

2 Have the children just listen as you read the story through once.

3 Read the story through a second time; have children use the markers to complete the activity presented in the story.

Read-Aloud Story

Look carefully! City shapes are all around. Place one orange marker on each square you see. Place one red marker on each triangle you see. Place one green marker on each rectangle you see. Place one yellow marker on each circle you see. Are you sure you found each one? Now, clear your math storymat. Do you see any shapes inside of other shapes? Pick three blue mat markers and place these markers on any three shapes you find inside other shapes.

Math Talk Tip + ~ x ÷ + ~ x ÷ + ~ x ÷ + ~ x ÷ + ~ x ÷ + ~ x ÷ + ~ x ÷ + ~ x ÷ + ~

- Before children flag shapes with markers, have them look at the mat and estimate which shape appears the most times. Then, after they locate shapes, have them compare the numbers of different shapes (e.g. the number of circles compared to the number of triangles; the number of squares compared to the number of circles, etc.).

Journal Extension

Have children locate and describe or draw any "shapes within shapes" or shapes inside of other shapes they may find in the classroom.

ACTIVITY B: ESTIMATION, MEASUREMENT

Target Skills
- size
- order
- counting
- estimating
- comparing numbers
- nonstandard measurement (height, length)

Materials
- copies of Math Storymat 8
- at least 30 markers of mixed colors per child

Steps

1 Distribute mats and markers.

2 Have the children just listen as you read the story through once.

3 Read the story through a second time; have children use the markers to complete the activity presented in the story.

Read-Aloud Story

Use your markers to measure and compare the heights of the city buildings pictured on the mat. Before you measure the buildings, try guessing how many markers you'll need for each one. Write that number on the door of each building. Then measure to see how closely you guessed. Which building is the tallest? How much taller is the tallest building than the shortest? Are any buildings the same height?

Math Talk Tip

Allow children enough time to estimate before measuring. Then, before they begin measuring, have children explain the reasoning behind their guesses.

Journal Extension

Have children place a marker in one corner of a piece of paper. Next have them line up nine more markers beside the first marker along the edge of the paper. Now they make a pencil mark beside the tenth marker. This gives them a "ruler" ten markers long. Have them look around for objects that match the ten markers in length. They may also look for objects that are longer and shorter than the ten markers. Children may draw, trace, or list the objects on their "ruler."

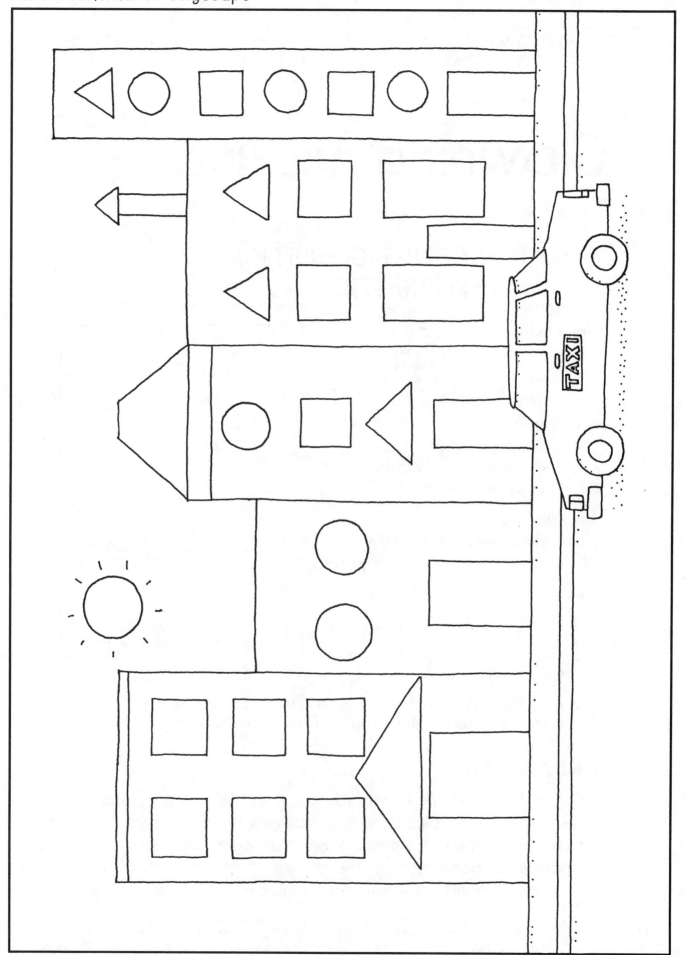

Clowning Around

ACTIVITY A: COUNTING, ADDITION, SUBTRACTION

Target Skills

Great for the whole class!

- ☼ size
- ☼ order
- ☼ patterns
- ☼ counting
- ☼ comparing numbers
- ☼ basic number facts (addition, subtraction, division)

Materials

- ☼ copies of Math Storymat 9
- ☼ 6 markers of mixed colors per child

Steps

1 Distribute mats and markers.

2 Have the children just listen as you read the story through once.

3 Read the story through a second time; have children use the markers to work out the situation presented in the story.

Read-Aloud Story

☼ Meet Bosko the Clown. You can help Bosko by using your markers as polka dots on his balloons. Bosko wants as many polka dots as possible. So use all of your markers to decorate his balloons.

If Bosko wants to use more dots on his big balloon than on his small balloon, how many different ways can you help him do that? Try it and see. Now, Bosko wants to have the same number of dots on both of his balloons. Can you show him how to do that?

Math Talk Tip + − × ÷ + − × ÷ + − × ÷ + − × ÷ + − × ÷ + − × ÷ + − × ÷ + − × ÷ + − × ÷ +

- Use a piece of chart pad paper to record number sentences representing the various combinations of two numbers totaling six. Have children describe any patterns they notice.

Journal Extension

Have children draw and describe how many ways a different even number of dots (four, eight, ten) may be divided into two separate balloons (sets).

....

ACTIVITY B: SKIP COUNTING, DIVISION

Target Skills

Great for the whole class!

- matching
- counting
- skip counting
- basic number facts (division)

Materials

- copies of Math Storymat 9
- at least 15 markers of mixed colors per child

Steps

1 Distribute mats and markers.

2 Have the children just listen as you read the story through once.

3 Read the story through a second time; have children use the markers to solve the problem(s) presented in the story.

Read-Aloud Story

Draw one more big balloon on a string for Bosko to hold. Now Bosko has three balloons. Take enough markers so that each of Bosko's three balloons has one dot. Clear your mat of markers.

Now take enough markers so that each of Bosko's three balloons has two dots. Clear your mat of markers. Now take enough markers so that each of Bosko's three balloons has three dots. Clear your mat of markers. How many markers do you think you will need so that each of Bosko's three balloons has four dots? Why do you think so? Use the markers to see if you were right. Clear your mat of markers. Now decorate Bosko's balloons any way you wish.

Math Talk Tip + − × ÷ + − × ÷ + − × ÷ + − × ÷ + − × ÷ + − × ÷ + − × ÷ + − × ÷ + −

* After children have distributed each set of marker dots on Bosko's three balloons, have them take turns describing what they did and how many markers they used in all.

Journal Extension

Ask children to suppose Bosko has eighteen markers to divide evenly among the three balloons. Have them write or draw journal entries showing how many dots would decorate each balloon.

In the Barnyard

ACTIVITY A: COUNTING, ADDITION, SUBTRACTION

Target Skills

- position
- order
- counting
- basic number facts (addition, subtraction)

Materials

- copies of Math Storymat 10
- container with 4 blue, 3 yellow, 3 red, 3 purple, and 2 orange markers per child

Steps

1 Distribute mats and markers.

2 Have the children just listen as you read the story through once.

3 Read the story through a second time; have children use the markers to "act out" the story as it unfolds.

Read Aloud:

Look at all the birds pecking at the feed in the middle of the barnyard! There are three fuzzy yellow chicks. There are two fat orange turkeys. There are three noisy red hens. There are three pretty purple finches and four sassy blue jays.

Uh-oh! The birds are beginning to scatter! Two of the yellow chicks run under the farm truck. One orange turkey waddles into the barn. One red hen scampers up to perch on the fence and two purple finches do the same. Each of the four blue jays flies away from the feed to a different spot in the barnyard. Where do they each land? How many birds are left to peck at feed in the barnyard?

Math Talk Tip $+ - \times \div + - \times \div + - \times \div + - \times \div + - \times \div + - \times \div + - \times \div + -$

☼ As the children first place the bird markers down and as they move them around on the mat, comment on the different ways the children have chosen to place their birds. Use as many position and order words as possible.

Journal Extension

Ask children to compare the number of each kind of bird that stayed in the barnyard vs. the number of corresponding birds that scattered. Also, if possible, have children watch real birds out the window for a few minutes and then ask them to write or draw what they saw.

ACTIVITY B: # COUNTING, ADDITION, SUBTRACTION

Target Skills
☼ size
☼ position
☼ order
☼ counting
☼ comparing numbers
☼ basic number facts (addition, subtraction)

Materials
☼ copies of Math Storymat 10
☼ 6 yellow markers per child
☼ a standard-size paper cup or 3" diameter paper circle (to represent bushel basket) per child

Steps

1 Distribute mats and markers.

2 Place a paper cup upside-down on the middle of each mat.

3 Have the children just listen as you read the story through once.

4 Read the story through a second time; have children use the markers to solve the problems presented in the story.

Read-Aloud Story

Six fuzzy little chicks are playing in the barnyard. They discover a basket turned upside-down (the cup). Five chicks climb on top of the basket while the other hides under the basket. Then one more chick climbs down from on top of the basket and hides under the basket. How many are under the basket now? How many are on top? Now all the chicks are under the basket. Without peeking under the basket, pull four chicks out and put them on top of the basket. How many chicks are still under the basket? Now, hide all the chicks under the basket again. How many are left on top to play?

Math Talk Tip + − x ÷ + − x ÷ + − x ÷ + − x ÷ + − x ÷ + − x ÷ + − x ÷ + −

As you work through this story with the children, allow enough time for them to find possible solutions to each question without feeling rushed. Continually ask them to explain the reasoning behind their conclusions.

Journal Extension

Ask children to write and/or draw a journal response to this problem: What if there were four chicks and half of them hid under the basket? How many could we see?

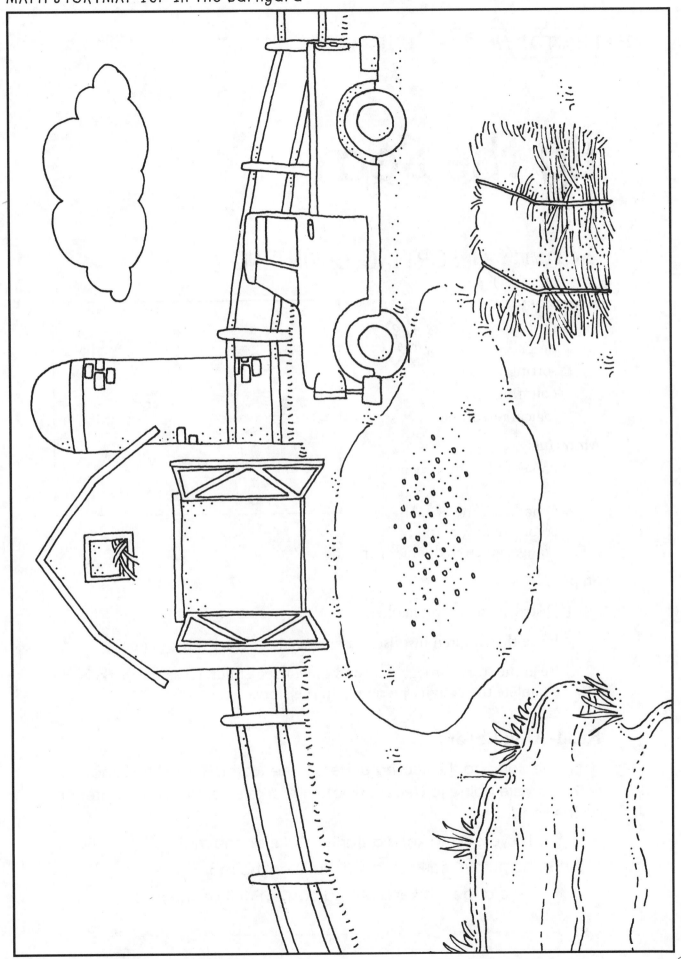

By the Sea

ACTIVITY A: SORTING, COUNTING

Target Skills

- ⚙ position
- ⚙ order
- ⚙ sorting
- ⚙ counting
- ⚙ logical reasoning

Great for the whole class!

Materials

- ⚙ copies of Math Storymat 11
- ⚙ 6 markers (one of each color: yellow, purple, orange, green, red, blue) per child

Steps

1 Distribute mats and markers.

2 Have the children just listen as you read the story through once.

3 Read the story through a second time; have children use the markers to complete the activity presented in the story.

Read-Aloud Story

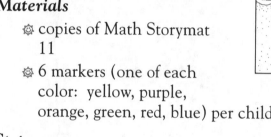 Welcome to the seashore! Here is the water. Here is the sand. You are going to decide whether markers belong in the water or on the sand.

The yellow marker is a starfish. Put it on the mat.

The purple marker is a raft. Put it on the mat.

The orange marker is a sand castle. Put it on the mat.

The green marker is a piece of seaweed. Put it on the mat.

The red marker is a beach blanket. Put it on the mat.

The blue marker is a fish. Put it on the mat.

How many markers did you place on the sand? How many did you place in the water? Could any of the items be found in <u>both</u> places? Which ones? Why do you think so?

Math Talk Tip + − x ÷ + − x ÷ + − x ÷ + − x ÷ + − x ÷ + − x ÷ + − x ÷ + −

☀ Help children notice if and why they made different marker placement decisions than their classmates.

Journal Extension

Have children list or draw three items (other than those featured in the story): one that belongs on the sand, one that belongs in the water, and one that could belong with either. Help children organize this information into a Venn diagram.

ACTIVITY B: PATTERNING, COUNTING

Target Skills

☀ position
☀ order
☀ patterns
☀ counting

Materials

☀ copies of Math Storymat 11
☀ container with at least 15 purple, 10 green, 8 yellow, 6 orange, 5 red, and 5 blue markers per child

Steps

1 Distribute mats and markers.

2 Have the children just listen as you read the story through once.

3 Read the story through a second time; have children use the markers to "act out" the story as it unfolds.

Read-Aloud Story

Pretend you find some shells and rocks and you place them in rows on the sand. First, you find three yellow and three purple shells. You place them in a row to make this pattern: yellow-purple-yellow-purple-yellow-purple. Next, you find four green and two orange rocks. You place them in a row to make this pattern: green-green-orange-green-green-orange Last, you find two red, two purple, and two blue rocks. You place them in a row to make this pattern: red-purple-blue-red-purple-blue. Now add more rocks and shells to make each pattern run all the way across the beach.

Math Talk Tip + − x ÷ + − x ÷ + − x ÷ + − x ÷ + − x ÷ + − x ÷ + − x ÷ + −

⚙ After children have modeled the patterns suggested in the story, review each pattern by pointing to each marker in order and repeating the colors with a steady, rhythmic beat. This will help children to "hear" as well as see the pattern.

Journal Extension

Have children use the markers to develop their own patterns. Then, have children write about and/or draw these patterns in their journals.

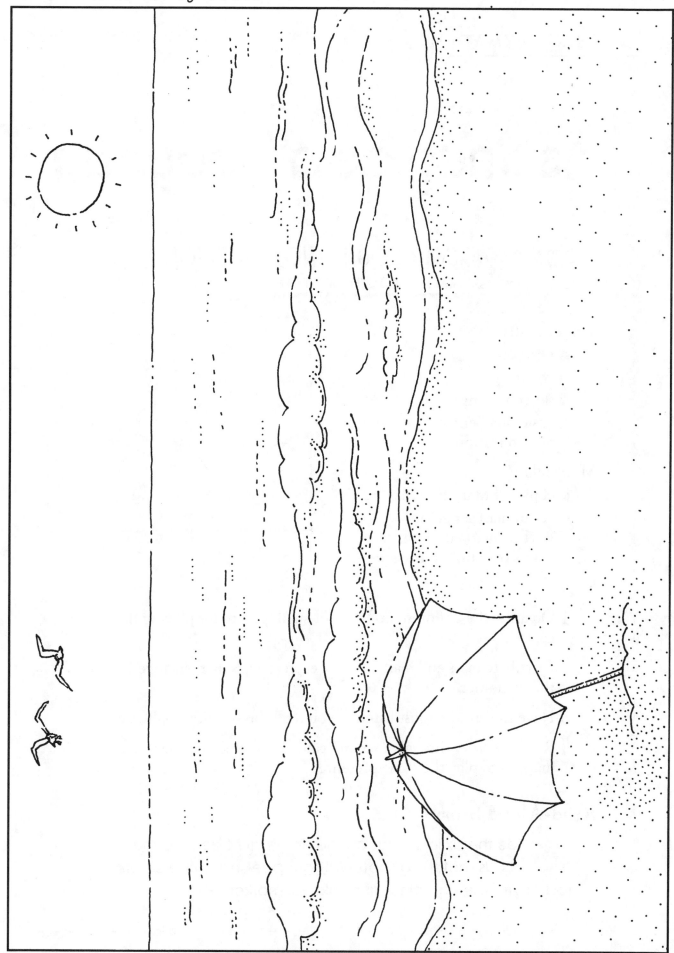

As Snug as a Ladybug

ACTIVITY A: SKIP COUNTING, ADDITION, MULTIPLICATION

Target Skills
- ☼ position
- ☼ counting
- ☼ skip counting
- ☼ basic number facts (addition, multiplication)

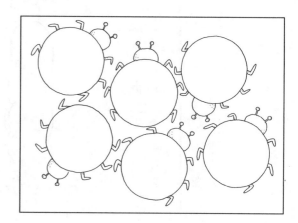

Materials
- ☼ copies of Math Storymat 12
- ☼ container (per group) with at least 20 markers of mixed colors per child in the group

Steps

1 Organize the children into pairs or small groups for playing the game.

2 Distribute mats and markers. Mix each group's markers together in the container.

3 Have the children just listen as you read the story through once.

4 Read the story through a second time; have children use the markers to play the game presented.

Read-Aloud Story

☼ See the six ladybugs on this storymat? Each ladybug needs matching spots. <u>Without</u> peeking at the colors, reach into the container and take six markers. Place one marker on each ladybug.

   Now take turns to play. When it's your turn, reach into the container without peeking and pick out one new marker. If the marker you pick matches in color the spot on one of your ladybugs, place the marker on that ladybug. If not, place the marker back into the container. Keep on playing until all of your ladybugs have two matching spots (or until you have no more new markers). Count the number of ladybug spots you have placed in all.

Math Talk Tip + – x ÷ + – x ÷ + – x ÷ + – x ÷ + – x ÷ + – x ÷ + – x ÷ –

   ☀ As the game progresses, model skip counting by continually counting the number of markers on each player's mat by twos.

Journal Extension

Ask children to show how many sets of two they could make with ten markers.

· ·

ACTIVITY B: PATTERNING, COUNTING, SUBTRACTION

Target Skills
   ☀ patterns
   ☀ counting
   ☀ basic number facts (subtraction)
   ☀ visual/spatial reasoning
   ☀ logical reasoning

Materials
   ☀ copies of Math Storymat 12
   ☀ 24 markers of mixed colors per pair of children

Steps

1 Organize children into partners.

2 Distribute mats and markers.

3 Have the children just listen as you read the story through once.

4 Read the story through a second time; have children use the markers to play the game presented.

5 Have the children play again (as many times as you or they wish).

Read-Aloud Story

Play this game with a partner. The two of you will share one mat. Together, place four ladybug spots of any color on each ladybug. Now decide who will go first. Take turns picking one, two, or three spots off the ladybugs. You must take at least one. You may take the spots from any of the ladybugs. Try to be the player who does not take the very last spot!

Math Talk Tip

At first children will tend to pick the most spots off the ladybugs. But, as they play this Nim-like game more times, they will begin to discover that this approach is not always to their advantage. As children move from random play to strategic play, ask them to talk about their strategies for winning.

Journal Extension

Ask children to use their journals to record the moves they made in the game. Show them how they may record the plays as a running subtraction number sentence (e.g., 24−3=21; 21−2=19, etc.) or suggest they devise their own recording method.

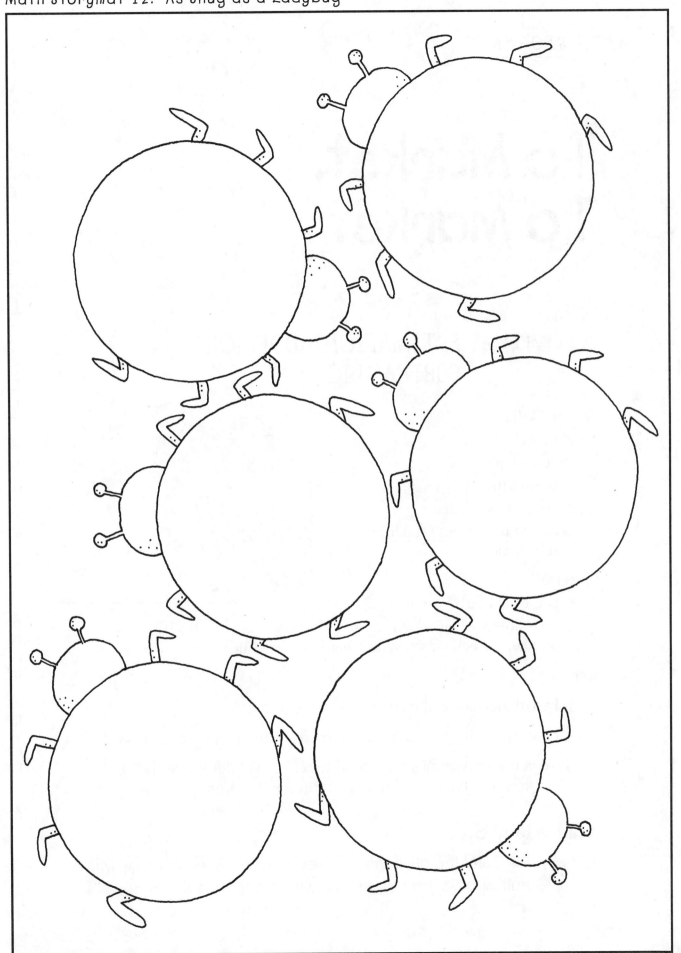

To Market, To Market

ACTIVITY A: ESTIMATION, ADDITION, SUBTRACTION

Target Skills
- order
- counting
- estimating
- comparing numbers
- basic number facts (addition, subtraction)

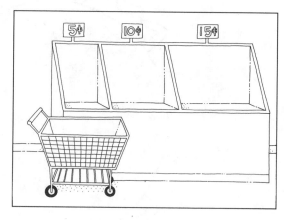

Materials
- copies of Math Storymat 13
- container with at least 12 orange, 9 green, and 6 yellow markers per child

Steps

1 Distribute mats and markers.

2 Have the children just listen as you read the story through once.

3 Read the story through a second time; have children use the markers to solve the problem presented in the story.

Read-Aloud Story

 Ms. Berry the greengrocer needs to fill the empty bins with fruit. She fills the biggest bin with orange peaches. She fills the middle-sized bin with green apples. She fills the smallest bin with yellow pears. How many pieces of fruit do you think are in each bin? Which bin holds the most fruit? Can you show how many more peaches there are than pears? (Hint: You may take the fruit out of the bins and arrange them any way you like on the table to show your answer.)

Math Talk Tip

- ☀ Have children explain the reasoning behind their use of the markers to make the number comparisons. How many fewer pears are there than apples? How many more apples are there than pears? How many fewer pears are there than peaches?

Journal Extension

Ask: If Ms. Berry has two bins the same size and needs to fill one with apples and the other with watermelons, which fruit will she need more of and why? Have children write and/or draw their answers.

ACTIVITY B: MONEY, COUNTING

Please Note

- ☀ In order to engage with the following storymat activities, children will need a working knowledge of money amounts up to 25¢. Spend time before and during the activity talking with children about how to subtract purchases from 25¢.

- ☀ If you wish children to work with money amounts totaling more or less than 25¢, simply cover the amounts printed on the mat with correction fluid, let dry, and enter new amounts of your choice.

Target Skills

- ☀ order
- ☀ money
- ☀ counting
- ☀ skip counting
- ☀ comparing numbers
- ☀ basic number facts (addition, subtraction)
- ☀ logical reasoning

Materials

- copies of Math Storymat 13
- 12 orange, 9 green, and 6 yellow markers per child

Steps

1 Distribute mats and markers.

2 Have the children just listen as you read the story through once.

3 Read the story through a second time; have children use the markers to solve the problems presented in the story.

Read Aloud Story

Time to go shopping! Pretend you have 25¢ to buy fruits for a fruit salad. Fill the smallest bin with yellow pears, the medium-sized bin with green apples, and the biggest bin with orange peaches. Now fill your shopping cart with any number of peaches, green apples, and pears that together cost exactly 25¢. You may choose either one or two different fruits to buy.

Now go shopping again. This time choose a different mix of fruits.

Math Talk Tip

- Offer children a chance to explain their purchase combinations to each other. (You may wish to have them make more than two trips to the fruit store.)

Journal Extension

Ask children to select a different combination of fruits they can buy with 25¢. Or ask them how many different combinations they can make.

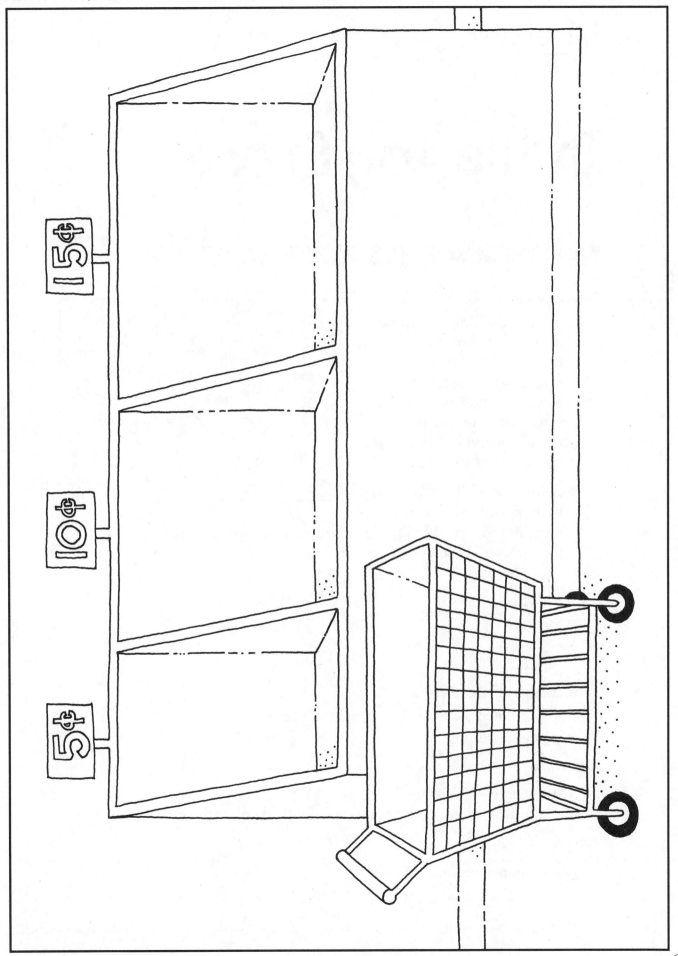

In the Toy Store

ACTIVITY A: SORTING, MONEY, COUNTING

Please Note

⚙ Children will need a working knowledge of money amounts up to $2.00 in order to engage with the following story mat activities. Spend time before and during the activity helping children add up purchases totaling $2.00.

⚙ If you wish children to work with money amounts totaling more or less than $2.00, simply cover the amounts printed on the mat with correction fluid, let dry, and enter new amounts of your choice.

Target Skills

⚙ sorting
⚙ money
⚙ counting
⚙ comparing numbers
⚙ basic number facts (addition, subtraction)
⚙ logical reasoning

Materials

⚙ copies of Math Storymat 14
⚙ container with at least 20 markers of mixed colors per child

Steps

1 Distribute mats and markers.

2 Have the children just listen as you read the story through once.

3 Read the story through a second time; have children use the markers to solve the problem(s) presented in the story.

Read-Aloud Story

Francesca saved and saved her money until she could buy a new toy. But now that she's at the toy store, she's finding it hard to decide what to buy. Francesca needs your help sorting all the different types of toys she likes. She likes toys with wheels. Place a marker on each toy that has wheels. She likes dolls. Place a marker on each doll. She likes animal toys. Place a marker on each animal toy. She likes games. Place a marker on each game.

Francesca has $2.00 to spend. Take markers off any item that costs more than $2.00. How many toys does Francesca like that cost $2.00 or less? Which toy or toys would you like her to buy with her money?

Math Talk Tip + − x ÷ + − x ÷ + − x ÷ + − x ÷ + − x ÷ + − x ÷ + − x ÷ + −

⚙ Some toys will have no marker while some can have more than one marker. Be prepared to talk with children about these cases.

Journal Extension

Ask children to write a "What Am I?" riddle about one toy from the store (e.g. "I cost more than $2.00 and I have wheels. What am I?").

ACTIVITY B: MONEY, COUNTING

Please Note

⚙ Children will need a working knowledge of dollars and cents in order to engage with the following storymat activities. Spend time before and during the activity helping children add up purchases totaling one dollar and change.

⚙ If you wish children to work with money amounts totaling more or less than $1.50, simply cover the amounts printed on the mat with correction fluid, let dry, and enter new amounts of your choice.

Target Skills
- ✺ money
- ✺ counting
- ✺ comparing numbers
- ✺ basic number facts (addition, subtraction)
- ✺ logical reasoning

Great for the whole class!

Materials
- ✺ copies of Math Storymat 14
- ✺ at least 10 markers per child (5 each of 2 colors)

Steps

1 Distribute mats and markers.

2 Have the children just listen as you read the story through once.

3 Read the story through a second time; have children use the markers to solve the problem(s) presented in the story.

Read-Aloud Story

☺ It's time to visit the toy shop to pick out a gift for your friend's birthday! You have $1.50 to spend. Use markers of the same color to pick out one or more toys. Be sure that when you add the prices together, the total is no more than $1.50.

Now make another choice of a toy or toys costing no more than $1.50. Use markers of a different color for the new set of toys.

Math Talk Tip

✺ You may wish to have children make more than two choices. Discuss with them how many different choices they could make.

Journal Extension

Have children use their journals to tally a receipt for each of their choices. The receipt should list the individual price(s) of the item(s) purchased plus the total amount.

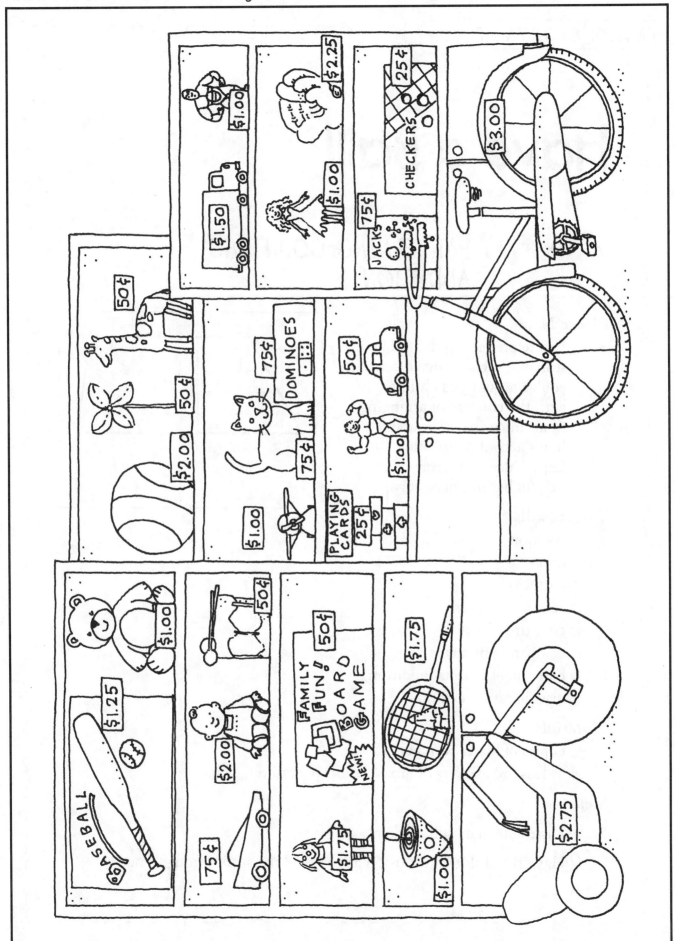

Have a Ball!

ACTIVITY A: PATTERNING, COUNTING, ADDITION

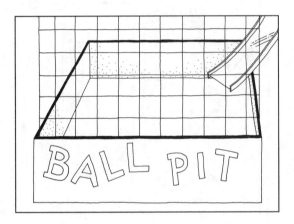

Please Note

◉ Before presenting the following storymat activity, make certain you've acquainted children with the concept of arranging items into sets, or grouping items according to color. Experience with arrays is helpful but not necessary.

Target Skills

◉ position
◉ order
◉ patterns
◉ arrays
◉ counting
◉ comparing numbers
◉ basic number facts (addition)
◉ visual/spatial reasoning

Materials

◉ copies of Math Storymat 15
◉ at least 30 markers of mixed colors per child

Steps

1 Distribute mats and markers.

2 Have the children just listen as you read the story through once.

3 Read the story through a second time; have children use the markers to solve the problem(s) presented in the story.

Read-Aloud Story

It's time to jump in the ball pit. But wait! There are no balls there! Use your markers to fill the ball pit with balls.

How many balls of each color do you have in your ball pit? You might try moving your markers around so the same color markers are easier to count.

Math Talk Tips

- Have children explain how they arranged their markers before counting them by color. *Ask:* Are your balls easier to count now, than when they were all mixed up? Why?

- If children are not able to easily arrange markers in an easy-to-count array, you might demonstrate how this can be done.

Journal Extension

Invite each of the children to take a handful of markers. Have them experiment with (and then color) two separate arrangements of these markers: one that is difficult to count by color, and another that is easy to count by color.

ACTIVITY B: PATTERNING, COUNTING, ADDITION, SUBTRACTION

Target Skills
- size
- patterns
- counting
- comparing numbers
- basic number facts (addition, subtraction)
- intuitive probability

Materials

- ◉ copies of Math Storymat 15
- ◉ 10 markers of mixed colors per child
- ◉ at least 20 markers of mixed colors per group

Steps

1 Organize the children into groups.

2 Distribute mats and markers.

3 Have the children just listen as you read the story through once.

4 Read the story through a second time; have children use the markers to play the game presented.

Read-Aloud Story

Place your balls in your ball pit. Count your balls to make certain you each have ten. Take turns with other players in your group. When it is your turn, reach into the group container and pick out one marker. No peeking to see the color! If the marker matches the color of a ball in your ball pit, remove that ball from the pit. If you do not make a color match, you must place the marker into the ball pit. Keep taking turns. Try to be the first person to empty your balls from the ball pit!

Math Talk Tip

- ◉ Each time a child makes a match and removes a marker "ball," encourage him or her to verbalize the subtraction process taking place, by stating how many balls there were before, how many are being removed, and how many are left.

Journal Extension

Have children tell if it was difficult or easy to empty their ball pits, and why. Or ask them to tell if the game will be different each time they play. Why?

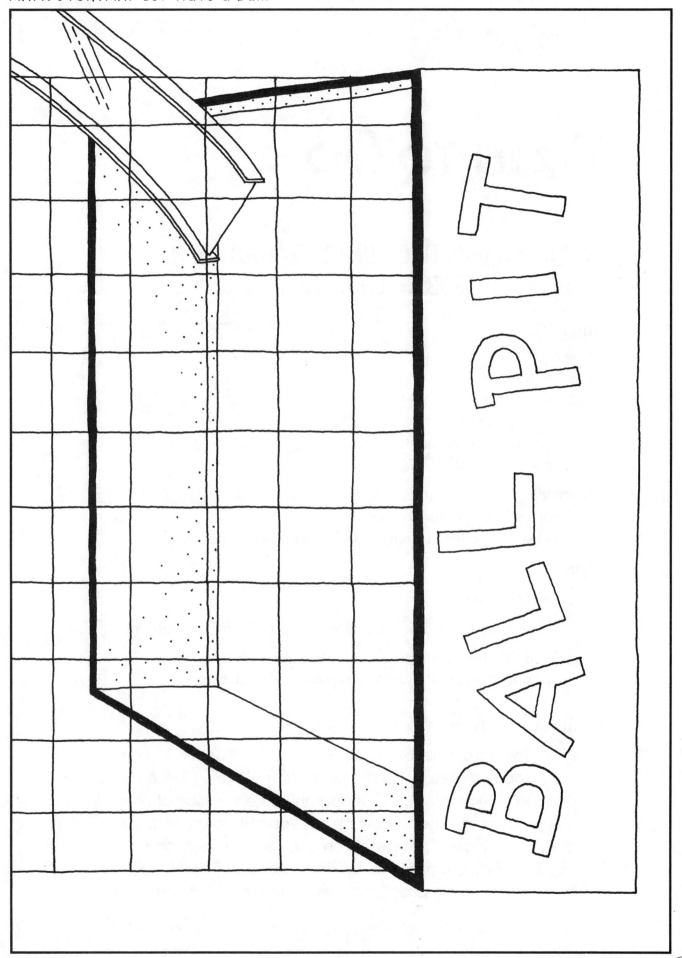

Pizza to Go

ACTIVITY A: SKIP COUNTING, ADDITION, SUBTRACTION

Target Skills
- position
- counting
- skip counting
- comparing numbers
- basic number facts (addition, multiplication)

Materials
- copies of Math Storymat 16
- at least 18 yellow, 12 red, and 12 green markers per child

Steps

1 Distribute mats and markers.

2 Have the children just listen as you read the story through once.

3 Read the story through a second time; have children use the markers to model the situations presented in the story.

Read-Aloud Story

This pizza is almost ready to bake. It just needs some tasty toppings before it's popped into the oven. Please place one red marker (pieces of pepperoni) on each slice of pizza. Count how many pepperoni pieces you put down. Now place one more piece of pepperoni on each slice. How many pepperoni pieces are there on each slice now? How many are there on the whole pizza? Now place one green marker (an olive) on each slice. How many olives did you put down? How many more olives will you need if you want each piece to have two olives? Let's pretend the yellow markers are pieces of cheese. If you want to place three pieces of cheese on each slice of pizza, how many pieces of cheese will you need to put down in all?

Math Talk Tip + – x ÷ + – x ÷ + – x ÷ + – x ÷ + – x ÷ + – x ÷ + – x ÷ + –

☀ Consider modeling how to skip count (by twos, by threes, etc.) whenever possible as toppings are placed down.

Journal Extension

Ask children to use any number of any color of markers to decorate a slice of pizza they would like to eat. Have them use their journal to draw that slice of pizza complete with marker toppings. Ask them to tell or write what each marker stands for and how many of each topping they used.

....

ACTIVITY B: COUNTING, ADDITION, SUBTRACTION, FRACTIONS

Target Skills

☀ position
☀ counting
☀ basic number facts (addition, division)
☀ fractions

Materials

☀ copies of Math Storymat 16
☀ 12 green, 6 red, and 3 yellow markers per child

Steps

1 Distribute mats and markers.

2 Have the children just listen as you read the story through once.

3 Read the story through a second time; have children use the markers to model the situations presented in the story.

Read-Aloud Story

☺ Count out six red markers (pepperoni pieces). Place these on your pizza so that each slice has the same amount of pepperoni pieces. Now count out twelve green markers (olives). Place these on your pizza so that each slice has the same amount of olives. Now count out three yellow markers (pieces of cheese). Place these on your pizza so that each slice has the same amount of cheese. Take your time with this last one—it may be a bit tricky placing three cheese pieces evenly on six slices! But it can be done!

Math Talk Tip

⚙ Have children explain how they decided to share three markers among six pieces of pizza.

Journal Extension

Challenge children to show how it is possible to share one olive evenly among six slices of pizza (by placing it in the center of the pizza at the point where all six slices meet).

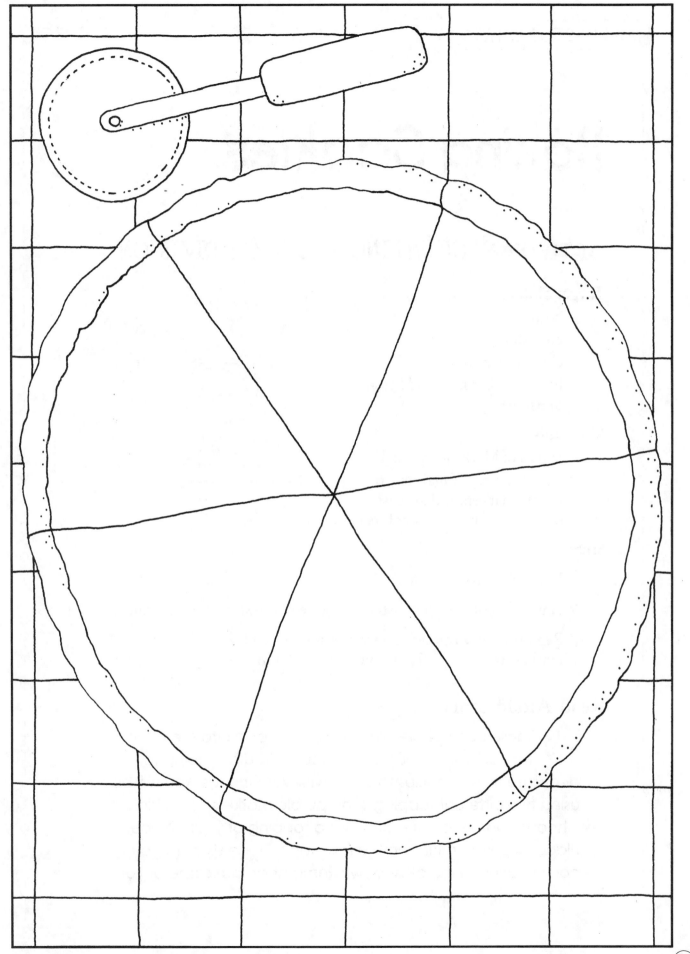

Baking Cookies

COUNTING, ADDITION, DIVISION

Target Skills
- ☼ position
- ☼ counting
- ☼ comparing numbers
- ☼ basic number facts (addition, division)

Materials
- ☼ copies of Math Storymat 17
- ☼ a large supply of markers: 6 purple markers and at least 6 of each of a variety of colors per child

Steps

1 Distribute mats and markers.

2 Have the children just listen as you read the story through once.

3 Read the story through a second time; have children use the markers to perform the activity presented in the story.

Read-Aloud Story

These cookies are almost ready to pop into the oven, but they still need your special touch. You are going to decorate these cookies to share with your friends. You will be using two different toppings. The purple markers are raisins. Choose another color marker for a topping of your choice. Place six purple raisins on the raisin box. Place six of the other color markers in the glass bowl. Remember that some of your friends like plain cookies, some like a little decoration, and some like a lot of decoration. Now decorate your cookies with your toppings any way you wish.

Math Talk Tip + – x ÷ + – x ÷ + – x ÷ + – x ÷ + – x ÷ + – x ÷ + – x ÷ + –

- ◎ Ask children to describe their second kind of topping. Have them explain how they decided to decorate their cookies.

Journal Extension

Have children each draw one large cookie and "decorate" it with different colored toppings. Pair each child with a partner. Invite partners to compare their decorated cookies. Have partners each record descriptive journal entries, using the words more and less to describe the differences between their cookies.

ACTIVITY B: COUNTING, ADDITION, SUBTRACTION, DIVISION

Target Skills

- ◎ position
- ◎ counting
- ◎ skip counting
- ◎ comparing numbers
- ◎ basic number facts (addition, subtraction, division)

Great for the whole class!

Materials

- ◎ copies of Math Storymat 17
- ◎ 6 to 12 markers of any color per child (not the same for everyone)

Steps

1 Distribute mats and markers. Have each child place his or her markers in the class bowl.

2 Have the children just listen as you read the story through once.

3 Read the story through a second time; have children use the markers to solve the problem(s) in the story.

Read-Aloud Story

These cookies need some decoration. Pretend the colored markers in the bowl are gumdrops. Count how many gumdrops are in your bowl. Now place the gumdrops on the cookies so that each cookie has the same number of gumdrops. Then put the rest of the gumdrops back into the bowl. How many gumdrops did you have to begin with? How many gumdrops did you place on each cookie? How many gumdrops did you have left over? How many more gumdrops would you need to add to the leftovers in the bowl so that you could give each cookie one more gumdrop?

Math Talk Tip + − x ÷ + − x ÷ + − x ÷ + − x ÷ + − x ÷ + − x ÷ + − x ÷ + −

- Help children discover that they were given different numbers of gumdrops to begin with. *Ask:* Who received the most gumdrops? Who received the least number of gumdrops? Did any students receive an equal number of gumdrops?

Journal Extension

Ask children to draw two cookies and then to use a brown crayon to add a total of ten raisins to the cookies. Have children then write number sentences describing how they distributed the 10 raisins (e.g., $5 + 5 = 10$; $10 − 4 = 6$).

Graph It

ACTIVITY A: GRAPHING, PROBABILITY

Target Skills
☀ matching
☀ counting
☀ graphing
☀ probability

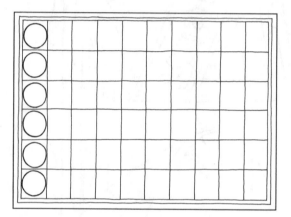

Materials
☀ copies of Math Storymat 18
☀ container with a large supply of markers (at least 10 of each color) per group

Steps

1 Organize the children into groups.

2 Distribute mats and markers.

3 Have the children just listen as you read the story through once.

4 Read the story through a second time; have children use the markers to play the game presented.

Read-Aloud Story

This math storymat is just like a piece of graph paper. You can use it for lots of different activities. Here's one you can try now: Place a different color marker on each starter box. Now take turns reaching into the marker container (*no peeking at the colors*) and pulling out one marker at a time. Place the marker in the first empty square above the same color on the mat. Keep playing until a tall column of colors reaches the top of the graph paper. Which color do you think will reach the top first? You can play again and again.

Math Talk Tip + – x ÷ + – x ÷ + – x ÷ + – x ÷ + – x ÷ + – x ÷ + – x ÷ + –

- *Ask:* Does the same color win the game again and again? Tell why you think this does or does not happen.

Journal Extension

Ask: How could we change this game so it is even more exciting to play?

ACTIVITY B: MATCHING, COUNTING, PROBABILITY

Target Skills

- position
- matching
- counting
- skip counting
- probability
- identifying adjacent sides

Materials

- copies of Math Storymat 18
- container with a large supply of markers (at least 100) per group

Steps

1 Organize the children into groups.

2 Distribute mats and markers.

3 Have the children just listen as you read the story through once.

4 Read the story through a second time; have children use the markers to play the game presented.

Read-Aloud Story

Cover each square on your graph with a marker as I have done here with my mat and markers. The colors can go anywhere you like. Now look at the mat for two matching color markers that are in adjacent squares—that is, two squares that share one side. On my mat, here are two matching color markers on adjacent squares. Now, watch as I reach into the marker container and pick two markers. If the markers I pick match the color of two markers on adjacent squares on my mat, I will pick up the two mat markers and place all three markers into the container. If I cannot find any adjacent markers that match the color of the marker I pick, I will place the one marker I picked back into the container. Now, you try playing.

Math Talk Tip + − × ÷ + − × ÷ + − × ÷ + − × ÷ + − × ÷ + − × ÷ + − × ÷ + − × ÷ + −

⚙ Make sure children understand that squares touching diagonally are not adjacent. Encourage students to use math terms such as "adjacent" and "subtract from" as they play. Also have them skip count (by twos) to keep an ongoing tally of the number of markers being lifted in one turn from a mat, or to find the total number of markers that remain.

Journal Extension

Ask children to make up a game that uses markers and a die and can be played with two people. Have children use their journals to record the game's rules and then try to play the game with a partner.

Notes

Notes

Notes

Notes